This guiding question has been something we've returned to again and again in all of our studies. This included studies in Art, Music, History, Geography, RE, Computer Science, PSHE and Science. All of the writing that you will see in this book is by our Year 7 friends, and has helped us to consider our answer to the guiding question.

For the immersion of our learning expedition we studied the LGSM group. This stands for Lesbian and Gays in Support of the Miners. During the 1984 strike the miners were against the mines closing because that was a big part of their community. The lesbian and gay community also supported the miners as they believed that they were a group that were being marginalised, just like the lesbians and gays felt they were out of place in society. These two groups of people were very different but became friends because of their shared cause. This showed us how a community can be made up of lots of diverse people from different backgrounds, but they can still belong together if they have a shared purpose.

We also studied maps of pit villages. We saw how one particular example of Whitburn Village changed from 1898 to the 1970s. We learned that like many other pits the village before the mine was rural and had a very small population with small dwellings. Then as the mine was developed, railways and roads were built and new areas were developed. The study of these maps has prepared us for the expedition because it helps us understand the clear link between the success of the pits and the villages that grew around them. When the pits were doing well then the villages were doing well, but when the

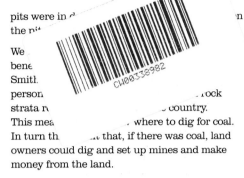

pits were in ____ ____ n the p__

We ____ bene____ Smith____ person____ ____ ock strata ____ ____ country. This mea____ ____ where to dig for coal. In turn th____ ____ that, if there was coal, land owners could dig and set up mines and make money from the land.

We also looked at boreholes from history. These holes (usually about an arm's width) drilled down deep into the earth take out samples of each stratum in order to study the ground. This might be done to search for coal, or to check the state of the ground before building on it. We looked at a borehole from Whitburn Yard that goes almost 200 metres down through the Magnesian Limestone and Yellow Sands into the Coal Measures. This helped to develop our understanding of the layers of rocks in the region. We also saw, by comparing boreholes from Felling and Whitburn, how the rocks dip down to the East due to tectonic plate movements in the deep geological past.

We followed this with three case studies, looking at the growth and decline of industry, the 1984 strike, and the impact of the pit closures on individuals and communities. Our writing in the chapters throughout this book details our learning from these case studies.

We hope you enjoy reading it as much as we enjoyed researching and writing it.

What do the communities of North East England owe to the miners?

It is worth first stating that when considering our debt to the miners, it is more than just North-East England that we need to consider, but all the UK and the world. The industrial revolution was a complete change in history. North-East England was the powerhouse of the country and provided coal to London, which in turn led to the UK being one of the richest countries in the world. It just so happened that the North East of England had the right conditions in the deep geological past to provide us with coal during the industrial revolution.

Coal was such an important fuel as it stored 3 times more energy than the equivalent mass of wood, supplies of which were running out at the time of the industrial revolution. To get this important fuel, conditions were dark and horrible, it was unhygienic and there were rats and coal dust to contend with. So we need to recognise the sacrifices the miners made so that Britain could develop.

Miners also formed unions to try to improve the conditions in the mine. This had a bigger effect of giving working people a voice, which is another thing that we need to respect the miners for.

Another important part of this question is the link between the pits and communities that grew around them. The pits were so important to the villages as they led to them being built in the first place, but more importantly they are also what made the communities so strong. For example when interviewing Jean, one of our experts, she said that the pits were the heartbeat of the village. An example of this was how the shop opened around times of the miners' shifts. Mining communities were often small but strong as everyone knew and trusted each other.

The closures of pits also taught us a lesson about what the communities of the NE owed to the miners. The closure of the pits caused many villages to decline as miners did not need a house near the pits and so many left in search of jobs.

Many ex-miners or people (mostly men) in mining families didn't know what to do with their lives as they had either always mined or expected to be a miner one day. This meant the communities had a lack of direction when the pits closed.

Unemployment and under investment in these areas has led people to high levels of drug abuse and crime in places like Easington. Without the mines, the sense of community had disappeared.

Whilst the mines were still open, communities in the village had a shared purpose, this meant that there was a sense of togetherness and trust. They have helped develop the North East during the Industrial Revolution and have taken their time to provide us with energy. For this we owe them respect as they have risked their lives for us. We owe it to them to continue to share their stories, remembering them for what they did.

The rocks of the Great North Coalfield

There are three main strata found in the Great North Coalfield. The oldest being the Coal Measures which surface in the west of the coalfield. Lying on top of that, further to the east, is a thin stratum called the Yellow Sands. Next to the East Coast is the Magnesian Limestone, the youngest of the strata in the coalfield. This pattern is called the stratigraphic order, and allows us to determine the relative age of each layer. The Coal Measures were formed roughly 300 million years ago in the Carboniferous Period by the peat formed in humid swamps. Then the Yellow Sands were formed from fine grains of wind-blown desert sands in the Permian Period.

Finally, the Magnesian Limestone which is made from minerals of the skeletons of dead sea creatures was formed around 250 million years ago, also at the end of the Permian Period from an ancient sea called the Zechstein Sea. We will begin with a close look at the Coal Measures, which bear the seams of coal that were so important to our region.

The Coal Measures

As mentioned, the Coal Measures surface in the west of the region and are between 313 to 309 million years. This stratum is made mainly from siltstones, mudstones, sandstones and between these layers are seams of coal. Examples of important coal seams in our region are the Five Quarter, Brockwell and High Main. The coal was formed in the Carboniferous Period in a swampy, moist environment. Britain was close to the equator at the time and there was around 10% more oxygen in the air meaning that insects such as dragonflies grew to tremendous sizes. Amphibians were the dominant land animal, but it is the plants of the time that are most important when it comes to coals.

When the gigantic trees and plants of this time died, their bodies and foliage fell onto the ground piling on top of each other they formed an important soil called peat. Since there was no oxygen in the water this organic matter did not decompose and over time the peat soil built up. Over tens of thousands of years the pressure from successive layers compressed the peat. The peat was transformed due to increasing heat and pressure to become coal. It takes around 10 metres of peat to make a 1 metre seam of coal. When looking for coal,

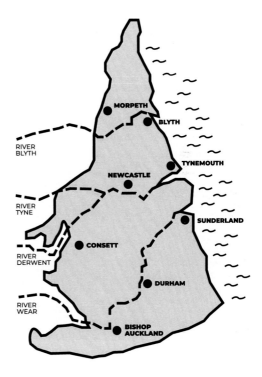

miners would seek out the thickest seams; made from huge amounts of peat, and the highest quality coal; made from coal that has been highly compressed and is very dense so that more carbon and therefore more energy is stored in each lump. Chance movements in the tectonic plates, and subsequent erosion meant that it was our region that was one of the places where these rich seams were brought back to the surface.

Yellow Sands

The Yellow Sands can be found in thin bands, often in the order of centimetres thick, near to the East Coast, although under the North Sea the bands stratum can be up to 65m thick. These rocks are often uncemented or weakly cemented and so are very friable, which means that they crumble easily. Under a hand lens you can see that these rocks are made from fine grains of yellowish sand. These grains came to be so small as they were in such a windy environment that the grains of sand would collide often and so would be weathered down to smaller, more rounded shapes. This stratum was formed between 300-250 million years ago during the Permian Period. At this time Britain had moved just north of the equator and was now a desert environment. The sands were wind-blown and were deposited into layers, these layers were eventually compacted and cemented weakly to form these rocks.

Magnesian Limestone

The world-famous Magnesian Limestone is found in the east of the coalfield surfacing in an unbroken line from South Shields to Hartlepool. The Magnesian Limestone gets its name from the high proportion of calcium magnesium carbonate (or dolomite) it contains. Its properties make it suitable for aggregate and the production of lime. The Lime Kilns at Marsden were used to 'cook' the limestone and produce lime for agricultural purposes.

Like the Yellow Sands, Magnesian Limestone was formed during the Permian period approximately 270-250 million years ago. What is now the North-East coast was at this time a hot and humid place with what must have been a very beautiful tropical body of water called the Zechstein Sea. This sea was populated with many tiny sea creatures. When they died, the calcium carbonate from the skeletons of these sea creatures built up to form a thick, rich, limey mud. Over millions of years, the sediment was lithified and was compacted and cemented into limestone (lime being a more common name for calcium carbonate). Mines near the coast were sunk down through the limestone to reach the seams of coal going out miles under the sea to reach the rich high quality coal beneath the limestone.

The Collieries

11

Chopwell Colliery
Gateshead

Chopwell Colliery had several pits with their own assigned name; Conclusion, Maraia, King, North, Pennyhill and Taylor. When they first opened they hired 2,185 men. The mines were very successful as they extracted 150,000 tons of coal per annum (year). At the colliery's peak, they hired over 5,000 men. However, by 1950 it was only 1,254. As well as the many pit shafts, there was a coal burning power station on the site.

In Chopwell, located in Tyne and Wear, a mining community grew because of the rich Brockwell and Five Quarter seams. Before the mines opened, the Derwent Iron Company was already mining the local iron deposits and coal had been worked on a smaller scale since the 14th century in Chopwell.

In 1781, the construction of the Chopwell colliery began, owned by Marquis of Bute. The Derwent Iron Company bought the mine in 1890. The mines here went on to produce 150,000 tonnes of coal per year in the late 19th century.

Before the pits came the village was just a hamlet (a small village) and was rural and green.

The community of Chopwell expanded over time because more people moved there to work in the pits. During the years of 1895 and 1896, first Wear Street, Tyne Street and Tees Street were built next to the pit. During 1899, Blyth street, Severn Street and Thames Street had been completed.

The men would come home and be filthy to the core from the coal dust since they were working so hard. Some miners would come home and be covered in blue scars from when they were cut in the mines and coal dust had got inside the wound. Some people still remember when their fathers were at work and their mothers hit their fathers pants off the wall to remove the coal dust.

Some miners would come home and be covered in blue scars from when they were cut in the mines and coal dust had got inside the wound.

The conditions in pits were generally unsafe but Chopwell did not suffer the same level of disaster as other pits. With that said, there were dozens of deaths over the years caused by problems such as falling rocks, a falling roof, electric shock and a shaft accident.

The mine has changed owners throughout the years and went into public ownership in 1947. Soon after this, in 1950, working on the Five Quarter seam was discontinued.

The mines closed on 25th November, 1966. The reason the mines closed is because of the amount of accidents leading to the work on the seams being discontinued. This had a big impact on the community and its identity. Today, many people in Chopwell still think of their village as a mining village but just without a mine. At the site now, is a nature reserve which is now managed by Durham Wildlife Trust.

Dunston Colliery
Gateshead

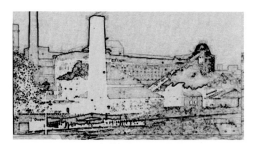

Dunston Colliery was located in Gateshead near the River Tyne. The mine was located here because the coal could easily be transported by boat to London. Soon after the colliery opened, the Staithes at Dunston were completed which made transportation of the coal even more efficient.

Before Dunston Colliery existed the land was rural, farmland and a lot of greenery. The people who lived there relied upon the rivers and farms. They lived in small dwellings (houses). The shallow coal seams had been mined away. This suggests that people had been coal mining before the colliery opened.

In the 19th and 20th century, Dunston became increasingly industrial. In 1874, Dunston Colliery was sunk and closed after just twelve

months of opening. The pit remained idle for 15 years and then reopened again in 1890. Upon reopening there were 400 men and boys that were employed to the Brockwell seam.

Dunston Staithes (a wooden platform to transport coal – illustrated above) was built near the confluence of the Team and Tyne rivers. This meant that the railways could deliver coal to the platforms from across the Durham Coalfield. The coal was loaded onto the ships, then transported to wherever it needed to be, usually London. By 1893, it was at a cost of £110,000 to allow coal from Gateshead to be transported.

At this time, the mines were very successful and productive, moving about 140,000 tonnes of coal a year.

Apart from a road bearing the name of the colliery, there is little evidence that the pit was ever there.

Throughout these more prosperous years, the village grew and the community became more established. The trams arrived in 1903 with a new school and churches. Within the community, social clubs for workers and miners opened in order for them to interact with friends and family after work, and they developed a strong sense of community. There were two social clubs for the men that worked in the mine.

That said, conditions in the mine were unacceptable compared to modern standards. During the time of the pit, dozens of men and boys lost their lives. For example, on the 27th February 1900, Jonathan Postle (aged 17) died as a result of a falling rock; tragic at such a young age.

After a period of decline, Dunston colliery closed in 1947 and this had a big impact on the community. 363 men and boys had to go and find different jobs, which was hard because all they had known was mining. The pit was abandoned in December 1948. Apart from a road bearing the name of the colliery, there is little evidence that the pit was ever there. The Staithes remain standing though, and are a well-loved and respected landmark, and a clue to Dunston's industrial past.

Felling Colliery
Gateshead

Felling Colliery, also known as Brandling Main, was one of the oldest mines in the region. Founded as a result of the coal seam under Ralph Brandling's estate, it was located where Mulberry Street stands today behind the town's modern day Metro station. The colliery was located here, not just because there were rich seams of coal beneath it, but also because there were also tiny farming houses scattered around the area which was already settled.

The history of Felling stretches over 800 years when the forests were first felled, giving the area its name. Felling Colliery began development in 1810. When the colliery opened in 1810, 128 men had gone down to work which was the main source of employment in the village.

At the time, there were two shafts sunk: John Pit and William Pit. John was known for being the oldest and largest colliery in the region.

Felling's community had strong bonds as they supported each other throughout the time the colliery was open. Over time, Felling had started to grow into 3 distinct villages. In 1834, it was noted that there also existed "a few neat houses and many cottages for the colliery which had small gardens attached to give an aspect of comfort to the village." At its peak in the 1910s and 1920s the pit employed almost 1,000 people, extracting upwards of 720 tonnes of coal every day.

Felling Colliery sadly closed in 1931. There was a loss of 581 jobs. When the mine closed it was really hard for a lot of families, because they had to find new jobs and it was hard to get by.

The history of Felling Colliery is heartbreaking. The mining conditions were similar to other mines; terrible. The conditions in all mines including Felling were really hot or cold depending on how far away from the door you were.

At its peak in the 1910s and 1920s, the pit employed almost 1,000 people, extracting upwards of 720 tonnes of coal every day.

Sadly a lot of men were getting injured while going down the mine. They would describe conditions as cramped, torrid and exhausting. For example, William Holle was a miner at age 15 for 4 years. He broke his thigh and was unable to work for 2 years because a waggon rode over his leg. He still suffered from dust inhalation throughout his life and said it made him feel dry inside; 'it gives me heartburn.'

The colliery suffered four disasters in the 19th century. The disasters were in 1813, 1821 and 1847 as well as 1812 which was the most major of all the tragic events. It was on 25th May 1812 when firedamp (methane) caused an explosion. A miner had come into contact with firedamp underground. The flame of his candle caused the mine to go up in flames in a huge explosion. Of the 128 working in the pit at that time 91 miners had died and the rest luckily made it out alive. Since the disaster had affected a lot of miners and their families, from that point on, the government required miners to use safety lamps when going down the mines. This makes the Felling Pit Disaster a really important moment, not just because of the awful loss of life, but also for the improvements to mining conditions that came as a result of the uproar from the public and from miners.

Heworth Colliery
Gateshead

Heworth pit was located 3 miles southeast of Newcastle. Heworth was one of the first large scale pits in the region and was built prior to the beginning of the industrial revolution. Without pits like this, the revolution may never have happened.

The site was located next to a public house on Albion Street (which is still there today). The reason Heworth colliery was located here is because new coal seams were found here such as the High Main. Before it was sunk and the community developed, it was an agricultural place and not many people were employed or living in the area.

In the early 1700s the mine was sunk under private ownership. Coal collected was then 1200 tonnes per day sent to London on boats and then to the London market.

Coal from Heworth and other such early pits was a driver for the industrial revolution, helping Britain to become prosperous. By 1819, new shafts were sunk on a new site called John Pit.

128 men worked in the mine initially and throughout its time, sadly 93 people died down in the mine. Conditions in Heworth Colliery were very dangerous and cramped. It had many instances of injuries including from explosions, rock fall and the heavy tubs which were used to carry coal crashing into people. Five people were killed in an explosion in 1826.

A whole community grew around the village with a football team, bands, blacksmiths, a school and a colliery shop.

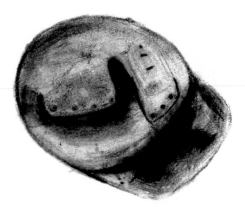

A whole community grew around the village with a football team, bands, blacksmiths, a school and a colliery shop.

In 1947 it was nationalised and the National Coal Board eventually closed the pit in 1963. Whilst other pits in the coalfield remained open for longer, especially the ones in Durham near the coast, other industries in Gateshead were proving more successful.

The concrete cap over the original pit can still be seen and the sheriff and deputies houses are still standing. Since the pit was opened so early in the coal mining times, it spent most of its life under private ownership, with 5 different owners reaching its peak in the 102 – with over 2000 men employed below ground and at the pit top. Today, there is a nature reserve near to the pub at the site of the pit, and other than the above there is little sign that there was ever such an important pit here.

Whitburn Colliery
South Tyneside

Marsden village was located in North east England, near to South Shields. It was built by the side of Souter Lighthouse directly next to the North Sea. This is why it was nicknamed 'The village on the cliff top'.

The village was developed here so the miners didn't have to travel far to the mine at Whitburn. Before Whitburn Colliery and Marsden village were created, the area was very rural. Back then, the cliffs were bigger than now. The village was at risk due to weathering and erosion of the cliffs.

The Whitburn Colliery had a very interesting history. In 1874 the shafts were sunk, but there were big problems. At first, the mine wasn't successful because it was flooded and they couldn't access any coal.

In 1877, new techniques were then used to line new shafts with iron tubes to prevent water ingress which was more successful and the mine started to produce coal. Despite these new techniques over 50,000 litres of water had to be pumped out of the mine every day.

In 1891, Whitburn unfortunately landed into money problems and was bought by the Harton Coal Board and saw growth from that point. At its peak there were 3,500 men working there. In the 1930s there were over 18,000 tonnes of coal extracted every week. A railway was introduced so they could transport materials and coal easier. The railway train was called 'The Rattler' because of the sound it made going through the village.

Working down the mine at Whitburn colliery was a very popular job for locals in the area. In the village there were other jobs available as there was a doctor's surgery, post office, school and a Co-op.

The sense of community throughout the village was very strong and people felt that they could trust everyone, leaving their houses unlocked.

The sense of community throughout the village was very strong and people felt that they could trust everyone, leaving their houses unlocked.

Community life in the village seems to have been enjoyable for the children. In Marsden Village they had two games they played often. One was the penny pressing game where children would get a penny and hold it on the train track until the train would come. Children would let go at the last moment and see how squashed the penny was. Whoever had the flattest penny won the game. The second game was the 'swinging cliff'; children would sit on the edge of a cliff and swing their legs as hard as they could and see how far they could get their legs to go out over the sea.

For the men down the pit, conditions were really cramped and dark, but there was a real sense of community there too as they all had to rely on each other.

By the 1960s the mine and the village had come to a close. The mine closed because too much water was getting in and it cost too much money to keep pumping it out. The village was demolished because the miners needed to leave to find a different job and there was the risk of coastal erosion destroying the homes.

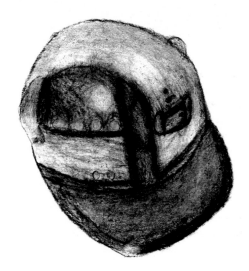

Blackhall Colliery
County Durham

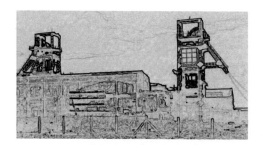

Blackhall is located in East Durham, 19km SSE of Sunderland. The colliery was there because they found coal seams such as; The main, low main and the Hutton. They needed coal because everyone needed the coal's energy to power factories giving the factory owners more money.

Before people came to Blackhall for the mine, it was very rural. Once people decided to come to Blackhall (because they had heard about the coal seams) it became more industrial and there were high levels of employment. Once the mine was opened, a lot of land was set aside for the pit top.

Blackhall colliery opened in 1909 under the ownership of Horden Colliers Ltd. When the mine first opened, there were just 240 people who worked there.

At its peak it employed almost 2500 people with an output of thousands of tonnes of coal per day. In 1947 the pit was nationalised, becoming owned by The National Coal Board (N.C.B).

For around 20 years the pit continued to employ thousands of men with high levels of coal output.

Miners were at risk for developing lung disease pneumoconiosis because of their exposure to airborne respirable dust. This type of dust includes extra fine particles that people can inhale into their lung tissue. As a result, the miners here and at other collieries also have an increased chance of dying of lung cancer. There weren't any specific large scale disasters, but 69 people did die at the colliery during its lifetime. The age of the victims varied from 14 to 64.

The sense of community throughout the village was very strong and people felt that they could trust everyone, leaving their houses unlocked.

In 1980 (1 year before it closed) it had 1353 people who worked there. Unfortunately, the village suffered economically after the closure due to the loss of jobs and industry. As a consequence there have been high levels of deprivation and also high levels of crime. Across the former coalfields, there are around 50 jobs for every 100 people, way below the 80 jobs for people in the South-East.

With that said, the closure of the mine had environmental benefits. Blackhall beach was black with coal dumped by the mine's conveyor system. When the mine closed £10 million was spent cleaning up the beaches due to all of the waste and pollution. Now the beach is in a much better condition. A pit wheel still stands as a monument to the colliery in the village today.

Easington Colliery
County Durham

Easington Colliery was sunk 14km South East of Sunderland in the county of Durham in 1899. The mine was placed here due to its ideal location between the coastal ports of Seaham and West Hartlepool, making it easier for the coal to be transported by ship.

Easington was not always an industrial area, before the mine was sunk, the area used to be rural. Farmers worked large amounts of land for their crops. Due to this, there were very few houses and jobs. It was mostly an agricultural society.

The mine opened, about 2 years before Queen Victoria died. Although the mine opened in 1899. Coal was not able to be mined until 1910 due to the repeated problem of water getting into the mine.

During the development of the mine in the 1900s, it employed 173 men which grew into 290 men when coal production started. The mine's most successful year was 1930, with 3,242 miners employed working the Hutton and Low Main seams.

The community of Easington was described as being one big family. As the mining community developed, the streets of Easington increased in size from only a few houses, to a larger village. As well as having more houses there were more shops and services. The community developed here as miners needed a place to live closer to their job. However some of the miners' families didn't want to move there so some miners moved to Easington alone. Throughout this, families had a chance to meet other families who then quickly became friends. Many of the residents here described the community as a 'trustworthy and friendly environment'.

Firedamp (or methane) a toxic gas that was of often found at mine posed a constant risk, and could suffocate and kill miners. In 1951, disaster struck. On 29th of May there was a massive explosion in the mine, claiming the lives of 83 miners, 2 of which were rescue workers.

The community of Easington was described as being 'one big family'.

John Wood quoted "After the explosion I went down the mine. My grandad stopped talking to me for a while due to the dangers of it." Only weeks after the accident, the miners returned to work, although Wood stated "The pit never fully recovered from the accidents."

In 1984, Easington was centre stage during the strike. The miners of Easington believed they were striking not just to protect their own jobs. "I want to emphasise the knock-on effects of the closure in pits and the loss of miners' jobs," Mike McGahey explained. There were many battles between men on strike who would set up picket lines and the police, who would attempt to break the picket lines to allow workers through, who wanted to work. Miners would run from the police and hide in their neighbours' homes to get away from them.

By 1985, the strike was lost and miners returned to work. In March the NUM voted to call off the strike, and the efforts were viewed as a failure. Indeed in 1993, the mine was closed making it one of the last mines to cease production. Many families had to move as there were no jobs for them in Easington. Even now Easington has not fully recovered. "A very difficult place to live." "A ghost town." "Everything's gone," said some of its residents when interviewed for television in 2018. More than half of the shops on the front street are shut down. Formerly the village had a bank and three cinemas. Now you find mainly takeaway food stores. Levels of drug abuse are high and some streets have now been demolished as not enough people lived in them and food bank use is on the rise.

Today the former pit top is a nature reserve, with the former cage that took men down into the mine the last reminder of a world that no longer exists.

Monkwearmouth Colliery
Sunderland

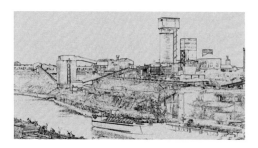

The Monkwearmouth Colliery was sunk half a mile northwest of Sunderland between the borders of Durham and Sunderland.

Before the sinking, the area was mostly fields, but it held many seams of coal hiding below. If the sinking was successful, it would come with many profits but it was highly risky. Two of the main hazards were that it was hard to get through the limestone rock at Sunderland and Durham and on top of that there was a high chance of the mine flooding due to ingress of seawater.

However, the rewards were attractive to prospective miners as it was known that there was a lot of high quality coal which would sell well and produce hot and long fires for customers.

Mining at Monkwearmouth Colliery was quite successful. The mine opened in 1835 and closed in 1993. There were also just over 700 people working there when the mine first opened. By 1910 the workforce had tripled to over 3,000.

The community at Sunderland were very close and they were like family. They treated each other so kindly and with warmth because they were really close due to the shared purpose that the mine gave them.

With that said, the conditions in the mine were horrific especially in the early days. There were 5 men who had fallen down a pit shaft and there was also an explosion that killed 7 poor men. The explosions happened because gases had leaked and exploded.

A miner James Lamb had said "my foot was in the tub to go down when the wind was so strong that I had to hold on to the staple so to save myself there was a chock to steady the cradle which forced it over the working side."

The mine owners at Wearmouth colliery were also ruthless. In our research, we read about an ex-miner called Albert Holyoak.

The closure, and the scars of the strike, had in part broken the close camaraderie and hugely impacted on the community.

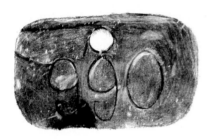

Albert's father worked at Monkwearmouth colliery and when the owners found out he had a son who did not work at the mine, they threatened to sack his father! This meant that Albert was forced to start working at the mine.

Strike action in 1984 aimed to prevent the closure of 20 mines, such as Monkwearmouth. However, on 24th November 1993, the mine sadly closed. The closure, and the scars of the strike, had in part broken the close camaraderie and hugely impacted on the community.

When reflecting on the closure, Albert Holyoak said 'These colliery villages, the community, they depended on the mines. When they closed, the roller shutters came down; Sunderland was a ghost.'

Since the mine was closed it now hosts a campus that is part of the University of Sunderland, and also houses The National Glass Centre and the Stadium Of Light across its former footprint. Barry Collinson, an ex-Monkwearmouth miner who now works at the Stadium of Light, which sits on the site of the old colliery, has said that this community spirit from the pit village has translated into support for Sunderland AFC, where a huge miners lamp still greets fans as they walk to the stadium.

Westoe Colliery
South Tyneside

Westoe Colliery was built in South Shields in 1909. The Colliery was located there because it was near the Bensham Coal Seam.

Before the Colliery was built here the land was unclaimed, anticultural and rural. The first time the land was claimed it was used as a place to build a man-riding shaft to go down into roadways below.

Westoe colliery has a very long and interesting history. It first opened in 1909 employing 427 men, but by the 1980s it employed just over 2500 workers. The mine had no major disasters but there were 7 known deaths over 84 years.

The mine was quite successful as mining was a popular job. Westoe was well served by train lines which made transporting the coal easier. In the roadways underground there was a train which took miners to the coal face so that they didn't have to walk long distances, therefore making it more appealing to the miners.

This led to a community growing here, with the miners within the community getting closer together, which is natural when you spend 8 to 14 hours in the mine everyday, relying upon each other. The community here was very close with each other, friendly and trusted because no one locked their doors.

Life was busy in Westoe mining town. It would have been a bustle of activity in the morning but quiet in the afternoon as in the morning the miners would be going to work and the milkmen/women would be delivering milk and that's also usually when people go and get food from the shop. The town moved to the rhythm of the pit.

The town moved to the rhythm of the pit.

Norman Strike, who used to work down the mines at Westoe, said conditions were terrible. The mines were damp, warm and crowded. This affected the workers because they were working in warm atmospheres, making them only go to work half clothed. There was coal dust and steam gas from the machines floating in the air, which badly affected many miners' health.

The mine sadly closed in 1993 despite the earlier miners' strike in which Margaret Thatcher and the Conservative Party won out, with miners returning to work and the eventual closure of the North-East's pits.

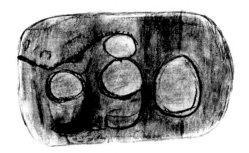

Vane Tempest Colliery
County Durham

Vane Tempest Colliery was established in Seaham, five miles southeast of Sunderland. It was established here because rich coal seams - the Five Quarter, Hutton and High Main - were located relatively close to the surface.

As it was also close to the sea, the coal could easily be transported away by boat. It was one of the last surviving mines but despite the miners' strike and a vigil, like all deep mines in England, it would come to close.

Before the mine was sunk there was not a lot of civilization in the area so it was very quiet with lots of wildlife. Back then the coast was 2 times further away than the site of the pit today due to coastal erosion. During its lifetime water was consistently pumped out of the mine, which made operational costs high.

Vane Tempest was operational for just 67 years. Vane Tempest opened 1926, and two shafts were sunk on the 4th of December 1943, one named Vane and one named Tempest after the surname of the lords of the land from previous years.

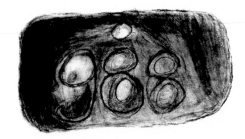

Vane Tempest was one of the last deep mines to close, with the community having put up a fight.

In 1930, there were just a few hundred people employed in Vane Tempest Colliery. By the 1950s it was close to 2,000.

Compared to many other pits, Vane Tempest was relatively free from disaster. The mine was still a dangerous place to work though, as there were many accidents that occurred quite frequently. Falling rocks were not uncommon, with 31 people known to have died in the mine.

The community surrounding the colliery were very closely knit and knew each other due to work as there were not many jobs other than those associated with the pit, or those that provided for the pit workers.

Vane Tempest was one of the last deep mines to close, with the community having put up a fight. When it was suggested that Vane Tempest may be closed by Margaret Thatcher's government, a passionate group of Women decided to hold a Vigil. The vigil was set up as a disagreement against Margaret Thatcher and the closure of the Mine. In Seaham a group of people wanted to support the miners. WAPC (Women Against Pit Closures). They wanted to set up a pit camp. It was in the middle of winter and if a vigil was going to be set up in the middle of winter it would have been protected by the wind, the rain and the snow. Easington District Council, which was already starting their own campaign against the closure of the mine, provided the women with a caravan, heaters and a portable toilet Despite this, the government closed the Vale Tempest mine on 4th June 1993, with the loss of 900 jobs.

The People

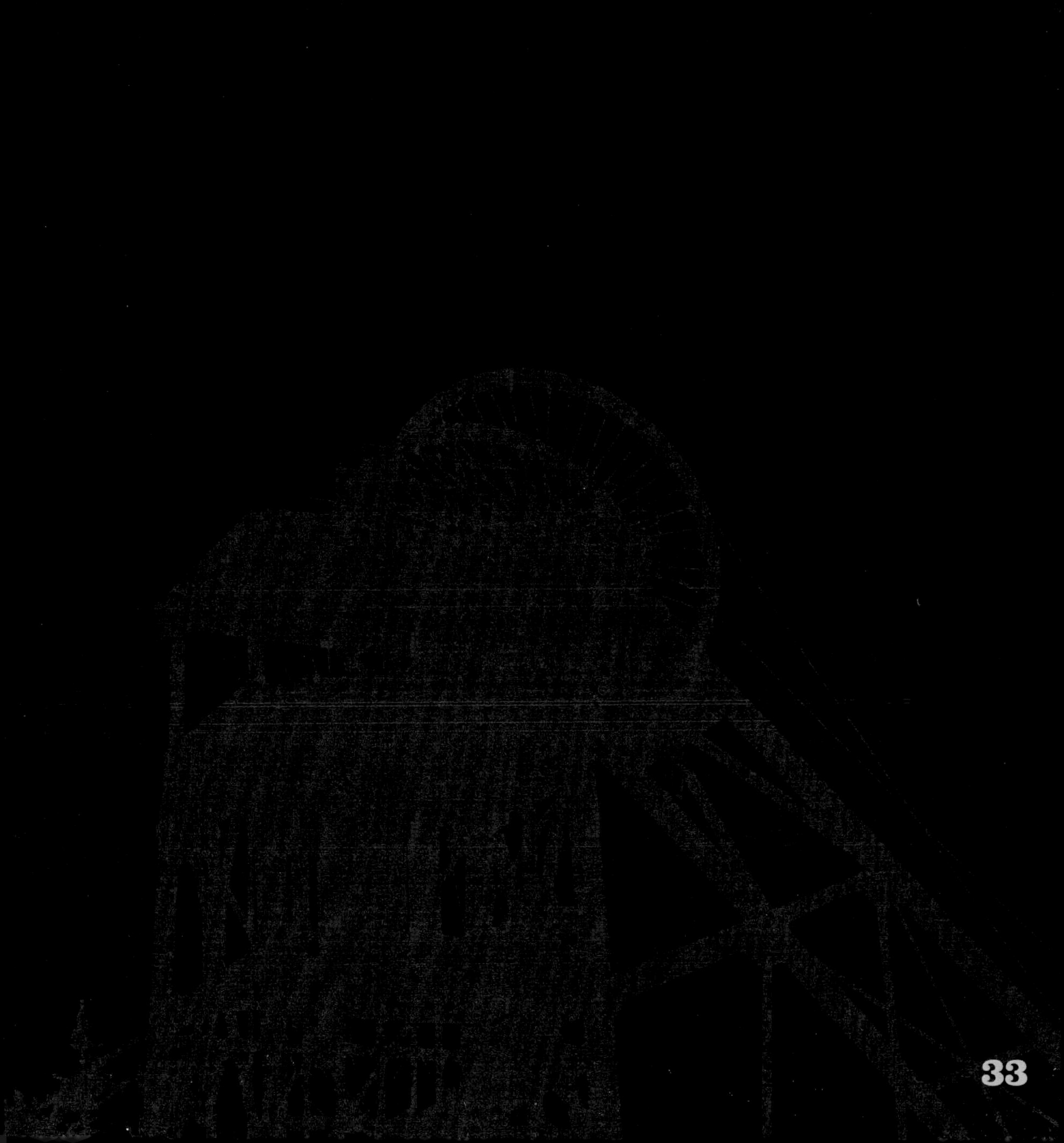

Norman Strike
Westoe Colliery

Norman Strike was a brave and rebellious young man taking part in the 1984 miners strike. Norman sacrificed a year of working and his life to take part in the miners strike. The strike was a period of time when many miners throughout the country refused to enter the workplace. This was a protest in the hopes of preventing Margaret Thatcher, the Prime Minister at the time, from closing Britain's mines.

The mines were to be closed on the 6th of March 1984 causing approximately 2000 jobs to be lost. The activists in question partook in activities such as travelling through the country trying to convince other miners to join their cause. During this time, Norman was jailed 2 times and arrested 7 times. He also recorded and published a diary recounting all of the strike's events.

Norman didn't have a very good early school experience; he hated it. He was born in South Shields, attending school until the age of 15, dropping out of school to join the coal mine. When he turned 18, Norman was able to go down the shaft and start working at the coal face. He described this work as 'dirty and dangerous' because it was tightly enclosed and there was always the risk of the tunnel collapsing onto him.

In the wake of the strike, Norman wished to attend university. Naturally, as he didn't finish school, people doubted his abilities but his marks continued to improve year by year and Norman went on to receive a teaching degree and become an English teacher. Norman encouraged young people across the country to really engage in school with his kind words 'Stick in at school, get the best GCSEs you can, do your A levels, go to university and then you have a chance.'

When the strike began in 1984, Norman at the time was working at Westoe colliery. Norman joined the strike due to him being a socialist and a part of the NUM (National Union of Miners).

'Stick in at school, get the best GCSEs you can, do your A levels, go to university and then you have a chance.'

When we heard from Norman, he expressed negative feelings towards Margaret Thatcher, who proposed the idea of closing the collieries. He joined the strike in the hopes of keeping the mines open so that he and his colleagues could continue to work.

Norman described the strike as a life changing experience that changed his schedule up, from the same thing day in day out to travelling the country to promote his cause. However, the strike was also very hard. There was no money coming in, the time he was able to spend with his two daughters, now 49 and 47, was sparse and the movement ultimately led to his divorce.

When protesting outside of Weymouth Colliery, police turned up but Norman was tired of the abuse and made the decision to charge toward the authorities. This led to an intense and aggressive beating which left many of the men with green and purple bruises.

After the strike, Norman moved to London to distance himself from the mining community. After arriving, he applied for a job in the Royal Festival Hall earning £300 a week. He was shocked at the income and thought he wouldn't get in. The interviewer asked him if he was a striking miner and Norman reluctantly said yes (thinking that he would never get the job).

Norman being dragged away by police at an NUM picket

He does not regret his involvement in the strike as the situation was very wrong considering the devastation and hardship it would cause for thousands of families after their main source of income was suddenly gone. After reflecting on his actions, Norman decided to distance himself from the mining community. He does still have an interest in workers' rights, strikes and protests, but due to the onset of rheumatoid arthritis he is now unable to protest in an active way. Norman is a very strong man with a challenging history, but overall the strike was an overwhelming, yet exciting experience for him.

Luckily though, the interviewer said his dad was a miner, and he agreed with the cause and he got the job.

Just after their defeat on the strike Norman was annoyed at the outcome, like most miners, but now he feels happy about the mines shutting saying 'it was a dangerous and dirty job anyway.' Although it was a thrilling experience participating in the strike, some of Norman's views on the situation have changed.

I personally think that meeting and interacting with Norman was very informative and interesting. He was able to describe his feelings about the situation very clearly to us and emotively. Speaking to him added to our understanding of the impact the strikes had on communities. We almost instantly noticed his kind nature and brave character. We would like to thank Norman for giving up his time to tell us his unique story.

Alan Cummings
Easington Colliery

Alan Cummings is a loyal, determined and patient ex-miner from Easington. He was the seam representative for the Easington Colliery and an exceptional member of the NUM (National Union of Miners). He was actually the representative of the seam for 30 years; he was someone who felt he could make a difference in his community.

He grew up in Easington, Durham in the North-East of England. During his childhood, his father had high aspirations for Alan and encouraged him to stay at school so he could take his GCSEs. However, Alan felt he wasn't academically inclined to stay on another year, hence his decision to leave school at the age of 15. Alan also told us that he could have worked in a local factory, and he could have got into the RAF as a cadet.

Alan knew what miners experienced and how tough it was for them. Growing up in a mining community was a different experience to how we live now. People knew everyone as if they were part of their family; they trusted one another. He grew up with the expectation that he would work down the mine. When he joined the pit he had to have checks to show that he was fit enough to work underground.

Many miners joined the union when they signed up to go down the mine. He told us 'When you started at the pit, the first thing you did, you had to sign on with the training. Obviously. And the forms, you know regulations... but next door you automatically join the union.'

Alan had strong opinions about the government's decision to close the pits. He used to, and still does, believe that we can mine and burn coal safely. He thinks that we, as a nation, should have made the most of the UK's vast coal reserves. The strike was about keeping the pits open for as long as they could, the strike members realised that the pits were going to have to eventually close due to exhaustion of coal or on safety grounds.

During the strike it was difficult for the community, but the hardest part for Alan was seeing the decline in the town of Easington.

During the strike it was difficult for the community, but the hardest part for Alan was seeing the decline in the town of Easington. When the strike was still going on, he helped people pay for their mortgage. He informed us that payments had been frozen until the strike ended. He then said that by doing this, it took a weight off their minds. He also mentioned the actions of others in the community, recalling how a Women Support Group opened the kitchen up in Easington Mining Colliery Club so families could get a meal 7 days a week.

Alan mentioned how the strike impacted him tremendously, it affected his health and was arrested multiple times. The strike was hard and it went on for months, but people didn't give up. After talking to Alan, I found out that the strike had a huge impact on him and his family. He found it rough. He only got £15 a week because the government thought it was enough. He used the £15 to get everything he needed to support his family. He kept on helping people during the strike.

The strike impacted him tremendously, it affected his health and he was arrested multiple times.

In an attempt to stop their comrades from going back to work, miners - including Alan - picketed (stood in the road in the way of miners attempting to return to work) and threw bricks and rocks at the windows of the buses driving them back to work. The buses that were used to transport the colliery's workers eventually had to be armoured with mesh around their blacked out windows.

After losing the strike, Alan felt defeated. He had campaigned for a year but in the end it had all been in vain. He went back to work when the strike finished because Easington Colliery stayed open for a further 8 years. In addition to this, he needed to bring his income back up after experiencing financial difficulties during the strike. Alan thought that the mines should have closed gradually to prevent power shortages.

Even now, Alan is still doing things to make a difference in his town. In the interview he told us that he continued to 'represent people at tribunals.' He did this in front of a jury and consultant. He is still engaged with the mining community because he represents miners. While speaking with him, whenever he talked about how he felt he sounded proud that he had done the best he could, and he used the word 'devastated' which made me think that he still thinks about and is affected by the mines closing. Alan informed us that he still believes that if there had been a national ballot called by the NUM in 1984 that they could have won the strike. He expressed the belief that 'if there had been a national ballot called in April 1984, I believe we could have won the ballot (support for a national strike) thereby bringing the areas that were working, out on strike.'

Alan was a great member of the community of Easington, and an important part too. Alan Cummings was a pleasure to interview and what we learned was really helpful. He is inspiring because he started out as a miner then gradually he worked his way up to the NUM. He showed real commitment to helping his community and resilience in the face of adversity. We would like to thank Alan for taking the time to talk to us.

Jean Spence
Vane Tempest Colliery

Jean Spence is a powerful, 70 year old woman who was upset by the way the miners were treated during and after the 1984 strike. This motivated her to become more directly involved in the 1992-1993 campaign against pit closures. In 1993 she joined the women from the Vane Tempest Vigil that protested against the closure of the mines. She had strong opinions on the mines, and believed the government was abusing their power to take revenge on the NUM (National Union of Miners).

She was born in Sunderland and raised in Seaham, where her dad worked in Dawdon Pit. When Jean was younger she was able to do well in school and went to college; in no small part thanks to the women in her family. At school she particularly enjoyed English, History and Economics and went on to study sociology at Middlesex Polytechnic. As a result, Jean had a strong sense of what was right and what was wrong. She was always one who spoke out where she saw social injustice. She was upset that working people never seemed to get what they deserved.

From a young age, Jean was interested in art and writing. She would draw landscape images such as flower fields and forests. She was a free-spirited young lady just like the many other women in her family. Like them, Jean was seen as a role model by her friends and family.

When interviewing Jean, she repeatedly mentioned that she had a love-hate relationship with the mines for many reasons, one being the fact her father had a passed away after suffered a heart attack whilst working in Dawdon Pit and sadly did not recover from this, and also that the pits had destroyed the landscape in her view, but she could see the importance of the pits to the communities around them. However, she pushed the negative aspects of her own feelings aside and was dedicated to keeping the pits open for longer. Jean did this because she believed the mines were being closed out of the government's spite and not the right economic reasons.

Jean chose to be an activist. She worked day and night to help the miners on strike receive justice.

She knew how much families depended on the income from the mines and felt the closures were too sudden and would have a devastating impact on the community. This shows how much compassion Jean has, as she has put other people's lives and wellbeing before her own happiness. Jean could imagine how much trouble it would cause to close the mines as she had come from a mining family.

Jean was inspired to join the Vigil of Vane Tempest, organised by a group of local women working towards putting an end to what they saw as the injustice of the pit closures. Whilst she was at the vigil, she and her colleagues worked from a caravan trying to develop other people's views on the strike.

Jean chose to be an activist. She worked day and night to help the miners on strike receive justice. The fact that people needed money to provide for their family after the mines shut really motivated Jean.

Vane Tempest was one of the last pits in the North East to close, in 1993. At this point, the vigil ended, leaving the community in despair. When reflecting on the area now, Jean described the aftermath of the strike and the later closures as if it had 'ripped the heart out of the community.' She suggested that the community has still not yet recovered from the loss of the mine.

Since the strike, Jean has reflected on her past of activism and she feels proud of what she has accomplished. Nowadays, Jean spends her time painting and writing, taking inspiration from the environment around her, proud of what she did in her younger years. Her paintings include landscape and still life drawings of what the area today looks like. She also has written insightful and powerful poems such as 'Twisted Seams', a poem about the 30 year anniversary of the 1984 miners strike as well as academic papers detailing the involvement of women in the vigil.

Jean was such an inspiring person to interview. We are extremely grateful to have such an amazing person in our region that stands up for what she believes are the right things. Its so hard to do what Jean does, especially at her level and accuracy. She deserves a substantial amount of respect.

Thank you Jean, we wish you luck in the rest of your arts career and, of course, happiness too.

Andy W
Monkwearmouth Colliery

Andy is an honest, open and strong minded man who never gave up at the hands of rejection. Once a miner, policeman and now a coroner's officer, Andy has struggled and fought during and after the strike, but that never stopped him. Brought up in a mining community, Andy followed in his father's footsteps in working in the mining industry, yet didn't devote his life to the mining community.

Andy was born in the 1960s, in Langley Park, but moved to Sunderland at the age of two and was raised in the Monkwearmouth mining community. When he was in school, his experience wasn't the best; he only obtained two qualifications. He said himself that 'I wasn't that smart but decided to stick in at school anyway.' At the age of 16, Andy began to work on the pit top in the supply yard, his Dad - a fire officer in the mine - having secured a job for him. Then a couple years later, he descended into the mine, where for 7 years (until his mid twenties) he would watch the belts, making sure that they weren't blocked and then supplying materials to the pit face.

Despite Andy being surrounded by pitmen, he never actually aspired to be a miner. Although he went down the pit, Andy never enjoyed being down there, but the camaraderie made it a better experience.

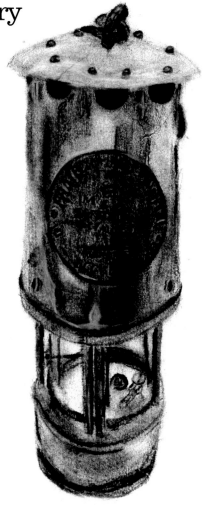

When Maragret Thatcher proposed the closure of the mines in 1984, Arthur Scargill, leader of the NUM (National Union of Miners) stood up for what he believed was right and initiated a strike by the miners. Andy's dad had a strong point of view about the strike and it encouraged Andy to follow in his footsteps again.

Andy supported the strike at first, as he believed that the union was working for everyone's interests. However, close to the end of the strike, his dad went back to work due to him being a fire officer and belonging to a different union. Andy felt that after this, he himself was treated differently by union men, poorly in fact, just because his dad had gone back to work. Therefore, three weeks before the strike ended, Andy also went back to work. Andy says that had he known the strike would end in three weeks, he probably would have held out, but still believes that he did what was right and stayed true to his principles. Some of his co-workers were upset with him, but in time this was forgotten.

Andy never went to picket during the strike because he did not fully believe in it due to the lack of a popular vote within the NUM. However, he did support his local union lodge. Andy's mum was the only person in the house working at the time and she had low wages. This meant it was a real financial struggle during the strike. He told us about needing wood to heat the home. Andy and his dad would cut down 4-5 trees a week to use as fuel for the fire. They also dug under the ground to get a form of peat formed from coal dust that they could use to put on the fire.

At first, due to being quite young, he viewed the strike as a bit of a holiday but soon it became a very hard lifestyle. He describes himself as being 'on the fringes of the strike' as opposed to his dad who was in middle management and a union. As a result of his dad's position in the union, he was supporting union members who were struggling.

Although he went down the pit, Andy never enjoyed being down there, but the camaraderie made it a better experience.

Following the collapse of the strike, and later in life, Andy made an unusual decision to join the police force, especially given the conflict between the miners and the police force during the strike. Andy could see that the pits were in decline and a member of his family suggested the police force as a career change. He first applied for the Northumbria force and didn't get in. He then applied to Durham and got to the final interview but sadly still didn't get in.

Despite this, he showed great determination and resilience and applied to Northumbria again and was this time successful, and that is where he worked for the rest of his career up to retirement in 2018.

He then became a coroner's officer, a job he has to this day. When reflecting years later, Andy mentioned that he thought he was very lucky, considering they lived in a big community near to the city centre in Sunderland, meaning he had many other job offers and paths he could take instead of mining. Whereas members of smaller mining communities had nowhere to go once they left their jobs - the mining community was their only source of money.

Speaking to Andy has inspired us to be as determined and as honest as he was. We would also like to thank Andy for giving his time to help us write this book; it wouldn't be complete without his story.

Alfie Joey
Thornley

Alfie Joey is a creative and talented man who experienced the anxiety of having a father on strike during 1984. Many of his male family members also took part in the mining strike. Since then, Alfie has created a children's book which reflects the importance of remembering our mining heritage which has been influenced by the impact of the 1984 mining strike.

Alfie Joey was born in the town of Thornley and his Dad worked at Vane Tempest Colliery. Many boys followed their dads down into the pits, but many pits were closing. Whilst Alfie's father was working hard doing back breaking labour in the mine, seven miles out under the sea, Alfie was dreaming of other things.

Despite being creative from a young age, Alfie Joey's childhood did not reflect this. In a pit village childhood it was unlikely you would be an actor, a comedian or an artist. Despite the brilliant encouragement from his teacher Mr Smith, Alfie never drew pictures seriously for another 30 years. 'For anyone wanting to become an artist, do it, as quitting art was one of my biggest regrets.'

As well as producing stunning artwork, he has inspired many people to start drawing.

For example, when he was hosting a comedy show, he asked people to draw a frog, then he asked them to draw it again but better, showing them that through effort and redrafting anyone can improve in any aspect of life.

Alfie believes that you can be what you want, whenever you want.

Later in life, Alfie published a stunning book 'The Last Coal Miner', which tells the story of a mysterious miner who rises up from the pit and enjoys fame and success until others start to become jealous, causing him to go back down into the earth. As we read this, we made links with our studies as we saw how it was important to continue to tell the story of the miners from our past.

Despite all of his family going on strike, as all the men in the family were miners, Alfie Joey himself wasn't old enough to go down the pit, nor take part in the strike.

However, he believes that being around his dad and uncles who went on strike provided the perfect role model of people who cared passionately about the community in which they live.

Despite this community spirit, Alfie witnessed the devastating effect the strike had on the miners and their families. During the strike, Alfie recalled that 'we didn't get any Christmas presents that year. We got bin liners with toys we wouldn't play with.' Alfie then went on to talk about how he had to go to the community hall to eat. This, to Alfie of course, was a little embarrassing but he had to do it as they were financially struggling.

Later that same year, he vaguely remembers his long march at the Durham Big Meeting which he remembers as the first politically related activity in his life. He saw key industrial figures like the leader of the Labour Party. Michael Foot. He remembers that he waved at him and remembered thinking that 'the old man on the telly was waving at me.'

Alfie left his village to train to be a priest. This took him to Liverpool, Dublin and London, and then he changed careers to become a comedian. Alfie was working in this field until he got a job offer to present live on BBC radio in the afternoons. By this time Alfie was already enjoying success as a stand up comedian.

After moving back up to the North East and being very successful with his radio program, Alfie started a family and got back into selling his art. He would later publish his book.

More recently, Alfie Joey remembered that same proud moment we talked about earlier when his dad was marching with his colliery banner when he was asked to do an interview for BBC radio Newcastle down at the Miners institute. 'As I walked in, the brass music playing, the surging of the rehearsing brass band (a sound sure to bring the easily moved to their knees), and the first banner I saw was my dad's. I was proud again.'

Alfie Joey is a very inspirational figure, who has contributed lots to our community. We would love to give a great appreciation to Alfie for

sharing his story with us at XP Gateshead. We would also like to appreciate his compassion for his heritage and willingness to share the impact his mining background has had on his view of the world. Thank you so much for sharing your inspirational story with us Alfie.

Despite this community spirit, Alfie witnessed the devastating effect the strike had on the miners and their families. During the strike, Alfie recalled that 'we didn't get any Christmas presents that year. We got bin liners with toys we wouldn't play with.'

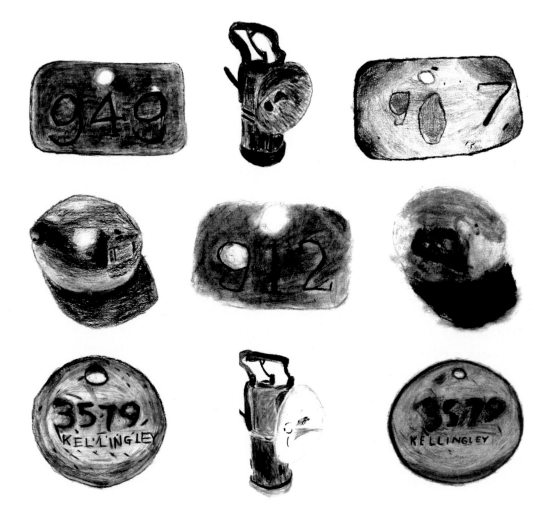

49

Geology Fieldwork

Thank you...

We would like to show our appreciation to all of our experts who supported us in this learning expedition.

Karen Daglish from Seascapes who supported us with the fieldwork around the former pit village at Whitburn and provided us with additional reading materials about the rocks at the coast.

Karl Egeland-Eriksen and **Simon Hendry**, our expert geologists that worked with us in the field and taught us how to read the rocks.

Vicki Johnson, **Dougie Holden** and the team from the National Trust at Souter Lighthouse who gave us access to the exhibition about the 'Village That Disappeared' and provided lots of useful additional information.

Penny Moody, our expert geologist that taught us about the Carboniferous Period and the formation of coal from peat.

Simon Woolley and the team at Beamish Museum, who guided us through time and an enquiry into the Mines and Collieries Act of 1842.

Alan Cummings, **Alfie Joey**, **Jean Spence**, **Norman Strike** and **Andy W,** without whose stories and wisdom, this book would not have been possible.

Brian Wilshaw Lovatt, father of our Principal, Mr Lovatt, an ex-miner, educator and life-long learner whose mining artefacts were the basis of much of the artwork in this book.

Finally, we would like to give our appreciation to the author **David Almond**. Our anchor text for this expedition was his novel, Kit's Wilderness. Not only is this a great piece of literature, which helped us with our studies, but it is a great piece of literature by an author from Felling. Just like in many former pit villages, the fictional Stoneygate has struggled since the closure of the pit, and Almond describes a wilderness in the spaces that the pit once filled.

We read this as an anchor text, because when the protagonist Kit's Grandpa was younger he was a miner. This links to our work on this learning expedition because Grandpa is sharing his stories with Kit as in turn Kit grapples with his identity and the ghosts of the past in a former mining village. Kit starts to become more interested and involved with Grandpa and his story, just as we did with the mines and members of the community we interviewed. If Kit didn't move to Stoneygate to live with his Grandpa, his Grandpa's stories would have been forgotten.

During our expedition, we have also enjoyed speaking to our relatives and experts about their experiences as members of mining communities and their memories of 1984.